Secrets and Sy...

North A...
Totem Poles

Molly Perham
Illustrated by Jo Donegan

Contents

What is a Totem Pole?	2
Thunderbird	4
Killer Whale	6
Bear	8
Wolf	10
Raven	12
Beaver	14
Shark	16
Mountain Goat	18
The Potlatch	20

FIREFLY BOOKS

What is a Totem Pole?

The Native Americans who dwelled on the Pacific Northwest Coast lived in tribes, or groups of related families. They believed that everything, from pebbles on the beach to animals, possessed a spirit.

Each clan (or extended family) traced its origins to a spirit, which had become their totem (symbol or crest). Pictures of these spirits were carved on totem poles, which were painted in traditional color schemes.

Each of the stories in this book belongs to one or more clans and has been retold here following a published version that was narrated by a clan member.

A Kwakwa̱ka̱'wakw pole from Alert Bay.

House posts & frontal poles

Some of the earliest totem poles were part of the structure of the house, used to hold up the roof beams. Frontal poles were positioned outside the front of the house and could have a door opening at the base. These early poles, dating from the 18th century, provided a prototype for the larger, and more familiar, totem poles.

Memorial poles

Memorial poles stood on their own, often in a clearing in front of a house. They were a symbol of a tribe's status, lineage, and wealth. It was usual for the top carving to represent the ancestry of the head of the house, while lower ones showed that of his wife's family and referred to particular legends of the family's heritage. A stranger could recognize which families were connected with his and where he might find food and shelter.

This Tlingit potlatch house has a painted front showing a killer whale, and frontal poles. The doorway is in the center pole.

Where are they found?

Totem poles were most popular with the First Nations (tribal groups) who lived on the Pacific Northwest Coast of Alaska and British Columbia. They include the Tlingit (pronounced **Kbling** -*git*), the Tsimshian (**Sim** -*shee-an*), the Haida (**Hide** -*ah*), the Heiltsuk (**Heilt** -*sook*), the Nuxalk (**Nu** -*hauk*), the Kwakwaka'wakw (*Kwah-kwah-***hooah** -*kwah*), and the Nuu'chah'nulth (*Nou-***char** -*nooth*).

The ancestors of these people came to this region between 15,000 and 10,000 years ago. The peoples settled inland by large rivers, at river mouths where they reached the sea, on flat land between the sea and mountains, and on the many forest-covered islands along the coast. Because they arrived at various times, these First Nations speak different languages, and have slightly different customs.

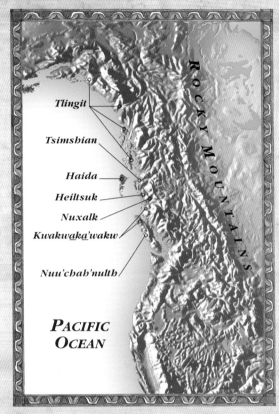

Mortuary poles

The largest totem poles are the freestanding mortuary (burial) poles that were erected in honor of a deceased (dead) chief, primarily by the Tlingit and Haida Nations. The figure at the top of these poles (such as the Tlingit mortuary pole in the shape of a killer whale—**shown right**) usually contained the chief's body.

The erection of a memorial or mortuary pole was an important ceremonial occasion. All these First Nations marked pole raisings with a potlatch (see page 20).

Thunderbird

In the legends of the First Nations of the Pacific Northwest Coast, thunder and lightning have great symbolic significance. Several stories tell of a giant mythical Thunderbird with supernatural strength that inhabited the craggy mountain peaks. When this immense creature flapped its huge wings, there was a terrific roar of thunder, and lightning shot out from its piercing eyes and beak.

A Kwakwaka'wakw head dress in the form of Thunderbird.

Each different tribal group had its own legend about Thunderbird. The Kwakwaka'wakw Nation tell how Thunderbird helped another ancestral spirit to build a large house. He then transformed himself into a human and so became the founder of that family. Others said that the bird provided food by swooping down into the ocean and grasping a whale in its mighty talons.

Thunderbird appears mainly on Kwakwaka'wakw and Nuu'chah'nulth totem poles. It is usually depicted with outstretched wings, and has curled horns on its head.

The Birth of Thunderbird

Toolux, the South Wind, always traveled north in the summertime. Feeling tired and hungry after a long day, he stopped to rest on the bank of a river. An old witch called Quoots-hoi lived in a stone cottage nearby.

Toolux said to her, "Give me some food, for I am very hungry."

"I have nothing ready," said the witch. "But here is a net. If you go and catch a little whale and bring it to me, I will cook it for you."

Toolux took the net, which was made from the roots of the hemlock tree, and waded into the water. He soon caught a little whale and brought it

back to the witch's house to clean and prepare it ready for cooking.

Quoots-hoi handed him a knife made from a sharp sea-shell and said, "Do not cut it across the back, but split it along the backbone."

But Toolux was in such a hurry for his dinner that he paid no attention to what the witch said and cut the whale across the back. The whale immediately changed into a huge bird and flew away into the mountains where she built a nest and laid her eggs.

Toolux and Quoots-hoi followed the bird and found the nest. They destroyed all the eggs except one, which hatched before they could break it. The chick that hatched from that egg was Thunderbird (left).

Thunderbird flew away to the top of another mountain that was covered with clouds so that no one could find him. And ever since, he has lived in the mountains making the thunder and the lightning.

Killer Whale

The sea and land animals that lived on the Pacific Northwest Coast formed the basis of First Nation mythology. Each family had a story of how an ancestor had a special encounter with an animal or spirit. As a result, they gained the skill to hunt certain animals, or the rights to hunt in a specific place, or wear a special mask, or use an animal as a crest.

A Tlingit story tells of ancestors visiting the undersea home of Killer Whale, where he gave them the right to use the killer whale as a sign of the tribe. The tribe was thereafter endowed with that animal's characteristics and its image was used as a crest. This right was passed on from generation to generation as a valuable possession, just like a house or a canoe.

A Tlingit blanket woven with a design that represents a school of killer whales.

Killer Whale can be shown held in the claws of Thunderbird. It has a long dorsal fin and short pectoral fins, and sometimes it also has teeth. It is used as a crest by all the Northwest Coast Nations.

Natsilane & the Killer Whale

Natsilane was a master carver, and the best spear-maker of the Grizzly Bear tribe. He tried hard to please his wife's family—on sea lion hunts, he was always the first to leap out onto the rocks to make a kill. By the time his brothers-in-law arrived, all the other animals had escaped into the water.

Natsilane's reputation as a hunter made his brothers-in-law so jealous that they plotted to get rid of him. Next time they went out on a hunt, the brothers paddled the canoe away and abandoned him on a rock. Only the youngest brother cried out for them to go back.

Natsilane tried to spear a sea lion to eat, but the spearhead broke off inside the animal and it swam away. However, the sea lions took him to their den, where he saved the sea lion chief's son by removing his own broken spearhead from the animal's side.

As a token of his thanks, the sea lion chief sent Natsilane home in an inflated seal-skin bladder. Natsilane stopped at a beach near his village, selected a piece of spruce wood and set about carving a killer whale. His first attempt failed to float, so he tried with hemlock wood, and then with red cedar. Finally he carved a killer whale from yellow cedar (left), which leapt into the sea and swam.

Natsilane told the whale to find his brothers-in-law and drown all but the youngest. When this was done, he ordered the whale to do only good to humans in the future, and so the killer whale became an omen of good luck.

Both the Tlingit and Haida Nations believed that great chiefs might return to life in the form of killer whales.

Bear

Marriages with animals, particularly bears, occur frequently in the traditional stories. The bear was thought to have a particularly close relationship with people because it behaves like a human and competes for the same food. It can walk on its hind legs, fish for salmon, and use its dexterous paws to pick and eat berries.

When pursuing a bear, a hunter carried out a special ritual, because he was killing a creature whose soul was akin to his own.

This Tlingit potlatch robe could only be worn by a man of high rank. The design shows the crest of the Brown Bear.

In the Tsimshian village of Kitwanga, there is a tall totem pole carved with the figures of a mother bear and her cubs. Its legend tells how long ago a girl from that village met a handsome stranger in the forest and found herself captive in the village of the bears. Other clans had their own version of the bear myth, but most of them followed this theme.

The Girl Who Married a Bear

One late afternoon, Peesunt, the daughter of the chief of Kitwanga, was picking huckleberries in the woods when she trod in some droppings left by a bear.

"Ugh," she cried in disgust, "what filthy, disgusting creatures bears are!"

Soon afterward, a handsome young man wearing a thick bearskin cloak came walking toward her through the woods.

"Come," he said, "give me that heavy basket. It is much too late for you to return home now. My village is not far from here.

You can stay there tonight."

He led Peesunt to his village, where a number of people were seated around a fire, all wrapped in bearskin robes. An old woman at the center of the group said, "Your insulting words have angered the Bear chief. He sent his son to bring you back and now you are to become his wife."

So Peesunt had to marry the chief's son and soon she gave birth to twin children (below left) who had human form in their own home, but changed into bears whenever they went out.

Back in Kitwanga, Peesunt's family were grief-stricken at her disappearance and her brothers searched for several years to find her. They hunted many bears all over the country until, at last, they found the cave where Peesunt was imprisoned and killed her husband.

Peesunt went home and was greeted with much rejoicing. And her children, though remaining human from then on, were able to to kill bears with ease, because they were related.

Wolf

Wolves were believed to have strong supernatural powers, but their spirits were harmless to humans. This was in contrast to the owl and the land otter, both of which seem harmless, but were in fact greatly feared because of their association with the spirits of dead people. A wolf is sometimes shown with flippers instead of paws—this is the mythical Sea Wolf, named Wasgo, from Haida legends.

Both the Kwakwa̱ka'wakw and Nuu'chah'nulth Nations claimed wolves as ancestors and impersonated them in their ceremonies. The Wolf Dance of the Nuu'chah'nulth—the Tlokwana— records the days when the wolves taught the people to live together in communities and gave them the hierarchies that were important in First Nation society. The creation story of the Nuu-chah-nulth tells how an ancestor visited the House of Wolves, where he was taught songs and dances. He thought he had been away for four days, but when he went home he discovered that he had been gone four years, and that he was still possessed by the wolf spirits.

A Nuu'chah'nulth ceremonial club used in the Tlokwana. The wolf is holding a human head in its jaws.

Why the Wolves Dance

The Tlokwana, or Wolf Dance of the Nuu'chah'nulth, begins when a group of young children, wearing ceremonial costumes, are kidnapped by men disguised as wolves. The kidnapping is symbolized by finding the children's ordinary clothes torn to pieces on the beach.

The parents of the kidnapped children are accused of being careless: "You should watch your children more carefully, then the wolves could not steal them." As a punishment, the parents are pushed into the sea.

Much feasting and merry-making follows this event, because it is forbidden for anyone to eat alone during the ceremony.

In the early hours of the morning, search parties go through the village looking for the children, tipping people out of bed and throwing cold water over them. When the search proves fruitless, preparations are made to attract the wolves by ceremonial drumming.

The drum leader climbs onto the roof of the clan house to watch for supernatural signs that the drumming should begin. In due course the sound of whistling wolves can be heard outside the house. The drummers stop, and the kidnapped children can be heard singing songs about how they have been captured by the wolves. The children are then taken away again.

Now the rescuers set out in canoes across the bay, armed with traps made of twigs and netting. After several feigned attacks and a great deal of hilarious jostling, the children are "rescued" and returned to the village. They perform the songs and dances that the wolves have taught them and their ceremonial costumes are burned.

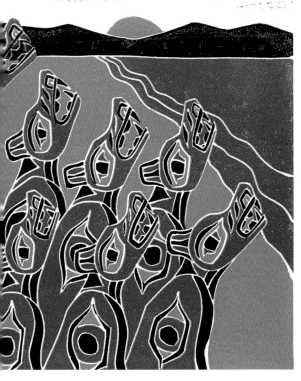

Raven

Raven is a trickster figure, or practical joker. His inquisitive nature and constant bragging get him into all sorts of trouble. He is extremely greedy and always looking for food. Despite his reputation as a trickster, Raven is also revered as the creator of the world.

One traditional legend tells how Raven grew tired of flying over an empty ocean, so he dropped pebbles into the water and these grew into the Haida Gwaii islands (otherwise called the Queen Charlotte Islands) that form an archipelago along the Pacific Northwest Coast.

However, the most widespread myth tells how Raven stole daylight. Not only does it illustrate his craftiness, but it also shows how he could change his form at will, even appearing as a human.

The figure on the top of this argillite chest, carved by a famous Haida craftsman, shows Raven as both bird and human.

How Raven Stole Daylight

When Raven was born, the world was still in darkness. Far up the Nass River lived a selfish chief who kept the light just for himself.

Raven thought of many plans for getting light into the world. Finally he changed himself into a hemlock needle, which then fell into some water that the chief's daughter was about to drink. The girl swallowed the needle and became pregnant.

When her baby was born (who was Raven), he gazed around with bright eyes. He pointed to some bundles hanging on the wall and cried for several days until finally his grandfather said, "Give my grandchild what he is crying for. Give him that one hanging on the end. That is the box of stars."

The child that was Raven

played with the box, rolling it around on the floor. Suddenly he threw it up through the smoke-hole. The box flew up into the sky and the stars fell out, arranging themselves as they are today (below).

Some time later he began crying again. Then his grandfather said, "Untie the next bundle and give it to him."

As before, Raven rolled the box around on the floor and,

after a while, he threw it up through the smoke-hole—and there was the big, silvery, full moon for all to see.

Now there was just one bundle hanging on the wall and so Raven cried for that. As soon as he had the box in his hands he uttered a raven cry, "Caw, caw," and flew out through the smoke-hole.

Raven tried to exchange the sun box for food, but he was only mocked for his efforts. So he opened the lid of the box anyway, and the sun burst out and rose into the sky.

The arrival of daylight transformed creatures into the physical forms they are today. People who were wearing the skins of otters, beavers, and seals turned into those animals. Those who were wearing nothing remained as human beings. They selected their clan crests in memory of their transformed animal companions.

Beaver

The beaver is often depicted chewing a piece of wood with its two large front teeth. Beavers can fell small trees by gnawing away at the base of them, and they use these to make dams and the lodges in which they live.

Beavers are common in the rivers and lakes of North America. Yet strangely there are no beavers on the Haida Gwaii (Queen Charlotte Islands) off the coast of British Columbia, the home of the Haida Nation. This story explains how it happened.

Beavers were often described as hoarding their stocks of salmon. The Tsimshian of Port Simpson tell of a huge beaver that attacked people who went fishing in its lake by splashing its tail to make waves and so drown them.

Coppers (plaques like this Haida example) were named and decorated with crest figures. This crest is obviously a beaver with its incisor teeth and scaly tail.

Raven & the Beavers

One day Raven was exploring an offshore island, when he heard an excited chattering noise coming from a clearing in the woods. Moving closer, he discovered a group of beavers playing a gambling game called lahal, which uses a number of marked sticks.

"Those beavers look plump and well fed," Raven thought, "so they must have plenty of food. Maybe I can trick them into giving me a meal."

Raven changed into a human and staggered into the clearing. "I believe you are my kinsmen," he said to them. "I have traveled a long way and am tired and hungry."

The beavers, following tribal custom, offered their kinsman food and shelter for the night. Inside their lodge, Raven sat by the fire to rest while one of the beavers went behind a screen and returned with a huge fresh salmon. It was the first salmon that Raven had tasted and he found it delicious. He decided to investigate the beavers' storeroom at the first chance.

Next day, the beavers set out to play lahal with some friends on another island. When they were gone, Raven quickly peered behind the screen and, much to his surprise, found

a lake teeming with fat salmon.

"Why should the beavers keep all this for themselves?" thought Raven. So he rolled up the lake like a blanket, tucking in the edges so that the water could not escape. Then he changed into a bird and carried the lake up into a tall pine tree.

The beavers were horrified when they found their lake was missing. Then they saw Raven and realized they had been tricked. They gnawed at the tree with their sharp teeth until it toppled, but Raven simply flew to another tree. They called on the wolf (center left), who dug at the roots, and the bear, who shook the trees, but it was no use.

Finally Raven flew away with the lake. As he flew, some water spilled out and made lakes on the mainland. He went along the coast until he saw a good place to unroll it. When the beavers finally found their lake, they settled beside it and never returned to the islands.

Shark

Shark, also known as Dogfish, is frequently found on totem poles of the Haida Nation. It is usually shown with a high, domed forehead and a large, turned-down mouth with pointed teeth. There are three curved slits, representing gills, carved on the forehead, the cheeks, or the shoulders. The fish can sometimes be identified by its tail flukes and its twin dorsal (back) fins.

This Tlingit defensive head piece has been made from wood and leather. It is shaped like a ground shark holding a frog in its mouth.

Sometimes the shark crest is carved with a woman's head on its back. This half-and-half figure has been claimed to symbolize the storm clouds and the sunshine. In the offshore islands of the Haida Gwaii, where the Haida Nation lives, bright sunshine can quickly turn into a rainstorm. Although the shark is an important crest of the Haida Nation, it does not have many long stories attached to it. There are, however, several short tales about the shark.

How the Shark People Got Their Crest

Some of the Haida Nation claim to have obtained their crest from a stranded shark that was rescued by a member of their clan.

The legend tells how a young man was walking along the shore at low tide, when he heard moans coming from farther down the beach. He followed the sounds and found a shark trapped in a shallow tidal pool. The young man released the shark into the ocean. In return the grateful shark taught him a chant that became the young man's personal song.

A Pacific Mermaid

One Haida legend tells how an old woman called Hathlingzo (meaning "Bright Sunshine") went into the countryside to dig up roots for food. When she had collected enough roots, she went down to the beach to wash them. While she was doing so, she disturbed a shark which was basking in the sunshine. In revenge, he turned her into a sort of mermaid—half-woman and half-shark (as shown below).

Fin-of-the-Shark

Another legend tells how a man called Rhadarhaerh left the Haida Gwaii after a family quarrel. He landed on the mainland near Cape Fox, and decided to make his home by a saltwater lake.

Rhadarhaerh hid himself and fasted for four days to see if the spirits approved of his decision. He ate only a medicinal plant called wo'oms or devil's club.

On the fourth day, he heard a dreadful noise coming from the lake. Then he saw an enormous fin and then a body gradually rising out of the water. Slowly a huge shark appeared before his eyes—it was a terrible sea monster.

Rhadarhaerh realized that the appearance of this gigantic shark, which was well known as Fin-of-the-Shark, meant that the spirits approved of his new home. And so he adopted the great shark as his personal crest.

Mountain Goat

Tlingit women wove magnificent blankets from the wool of the mountain goat. The animal's curved black horns were used to make spoons with delicately carved handles. Mountain goats live on the slopes of mountains along the coast of British Columbia. When the weather conditions become really severe, they descend to the valleys.

The mountain goat is found mainly on northern totem poles. It is easily recognized by the two slender curved horns and its small hoofed feet.

A famous Tsimshian legend tells how the mountain goats took revenge on the people of Temlaxam for treating the remains of the dead goats disrespectfully. It also explains why the mountain goat has red stripes on each shoulder. There are many tales of how families were killed by angry animals after their bones were disturbed.

This magnificent horn spoon has been carved from two pieces of mountain goat's horn. It was made by a man of the Haida Nation.

The Mountain Goats' Revenge

Around the village of Temlaxam on the Skeena River there were many goats, which the men hunted to provide food for their families. When the meat had been prepared for eating, the children played games with the skulls, putting them on their heads as if they were masks and then dancing around and singing. In the mountains the goats were aware that the children were making fun of their bones and they were offended by it.

At the end of one hunt, a young man found a small goat kid and took it back to the village to look after it. That evening, as they sat around the campfire, one of the hunters seized the little goat to have some fun with it and he threw it into the flames.

The young man sprang toward the fire and rescued the kid. He brushed the cinders off its coat and painted a red ochre stripe on each shoulder before setting it free. The little goat returned to its home in the mountains and told the other goats what had happened.

The mountain goats decided to take revenge (below). One of them turned himself into a human and invited all the men of the village to a feast. As they arrived, the young man who had shown kindness to the kid was taken to one side and the others were seated at the rear of the house.

A splendid meal was put before the guests and when they had finished eating, the singing and dancing began. The guests relaxed and enjoyed themselves. Everything was just as they expected, and there was nothing to arouse their suspicions.

Then, during the last dance, the chief goat hit the ground hard with his hooves and the house was split in half. As the guests stepped out into the dark they slipped right down into a precipice outside the door. Only the young man who had befriended the little goat survived.

The Potlatch

Potlatches are held to mark many important occasions. These can include the naming of a child, the coming of age of a chief's daughter, a marriage, the taking of an additional name by a chief that gives him more prestige, a memorial ceremony for a dead chief, or the raising of a totem pole. The important part is that the occasion happens before witnesses and is accompanied by feasting and the giving of gifts. A chief who is generous, providing lavish gifts and hospitality, is highly thought of by his clan and by neighboring villages.

Potlatch hats were only worn by chiefs. The eight rings on this hat (of unknown origin) shows that its owner had given eight successful potlatches.

The plan of events

Potlatches have a set plan of events. A modern Kwakwa̱ka̱'wakw potlatch lasts 12 to 14 hours, but in the past, they could go on for days.

A potlatch always starts with a mourning session: the potlatch giver asks women to come before the assembled chiefs and pay tribute to those who have died recently and their ancestors.

If a copper is to be sold or transferred, this is done next. This is a very solemn event. Coppers were used as an indication of wealth—they

A Kwakwaka'wakw chief, Willie Seaweed, in his regalia. It includes a copper, worn at his waist.

generally were valued at the same cost as the number of blankets given away at the potlatch. To throw one down in front of a chief was a great insult.

If a marriage ceremony is performed, this happens next. Then comes the great feast, including the *'tseka* ceremony when cedar bark head dresses are distributed to the chiefs, feast songs are sung and ceremonial dances —the *hamat'sa* and the *Ḥa'sala*—are performed.

Then guests join in *am'lala*, or fun dances. Lastly gifts and money are given to the guests in order of rank.